DARK CITY

Books by Charles Bernstein

A Poetics (Harvard University Press, 1992)

Rough Trades (Sun & Moon Press, 1991)

The Absent Father in Dumbo (Zasterle, 1990)

The Nude Formalism, with Susan Bee
(Sun & Moon Press, 1989)

The Sophist (Sun & Moon Press, 1987)

Veil (Xexoxial Editions, 1987)

Content's Dream: Essays 1975–1984
(Sun & Moon Press, 1986; 1994)

Resistance (Awede Press, 1983)

Islets/Irritations (Jordan Davies, 1983;
reprinted, Roof Books, 1992)

Stigma (Station Hill Press, 1981)

The Occurrence of Tune, with Susan Bee [Laufer]
(Segue, 1981)

Disfrutes (Potes and Poets Press, 1981)

Controlling Interests (Roof Books, 1980)

Legend, with Bruce Andrews, Ray DiPalma,
Steve McCaffery, and Ron Silliman
(L=A=N=G=U=A=G=E/Segue, 1980)

Senses of Responsibility (Tuumba Press, 1979;
reprinted, Paradigm Press, 1989)

Poetic Justice (Pod Books, 1979)

Shade (Sun & Moon Press, 1978)

Parsing (Asylum's Press, 1976)

Editor

The Politics of Poetic Form: Poetry and Public Policy (Roof, 1990)

Patterns/Contexts/Time, with Phillip Foss (Tyuonyi, 1990)

L=A=N=G=U=A=G=E, with Bruce Andrews (1978–1981)

DARK CITY

by

Charles Bernstein

SUN &
MOON

CLASSICS

48

LOS ANGELES
SUN & MOON PRESS
1994

Sun & Moon Press
A Program of The Contemporary Arts Educational Project, Inc.
a nonprofit corporation
6026 Wilshire Boulevard, Los Angeles, California 90036

This edition first published in paperback in 1994 by Sun & Moon Press
10 9 8 7 6 5 4 3 2 1
FIRST EDITION
© Charles Bernstein, 1994
All rights reserved

Some of these poems first appeared in *Avec, Big Allis, Caliban,
Conjunctions, Contemporanea, Fragmente, Generator, Hambone, O-blek,
Rethinking Marxism, Sulfur, Verse,* and *The Best American Poetry 1992.*
The author wishes to express his thanks to the editors:
Cydney Chadwick, Melanie Neilson and Jessica Grim, Lawrence Smith, Bradford
Morrow, Thomas McEvilley, Anthony Mellors and Andrew Lawson, John Byrum,
Nathaniel Mackey, Peter Gizzi and Connell McGrath, Jack Amariglio and Harriet
Fraad, Jerome McGann, Susan Schultz, and Charles Simic. Thanks also to the
New York Foundation for the Arts for a Poetry Fellowhip in 1990 and to
Douglas Messerli and Susan Bee.

This book was made possible, in part, through an operational grant from the
Andrew W. Mellon Foundation and through contributions to
The Contemporary Arts Educational Project, Inc.,
a nonprofit corporation.

Cover: Georgia O'Keeffe, *Street, New York, No. 1*
Design: Katie Messborn
Typography: Guy Bennett

LIBRARY OF CONGRESS CATALOGING IN PUBLICATION DATA
Bernstein, Charles
Dark City
p. cm — (Sun & Moon Classics: 48)
ISBN: 1-55713-162-7
I. Title. II. Series.
811'.54—dc20

Printed in the United States of America on acid-free paper.

Contents

The Lives of the Toll Takers

There appears to be a receiver off the hook. Not that

you care.

      Beside the gloves resided a hat and two

pinky rings, for which no

finger was ever found. Largesse

      with no release became, after

not too long, atrophied, incendiary,

        stupefying. Difference or

differance: it's

the distinction between hauling junk and

removing rubbish, while

I, needless not to say, take

  out the garbage

    (pragmatism)

       ·

Phone again, phone again jiggity jig.

  I figured

they do good eggs here.

Funny $: making a killing on

junk bonds and living to peddle the tale

(victimless rime)

.

(Laughing all the way to the Swiss bank where I put my money
in gold bars
[the prison house of language]
.) Simplicity is not

the

same as simplistic.

Sullen

supposition, salacious conjecture, slurpy ded

uction.

"A picture

[fixture]

is worth more than a thousand words":

With this

sally, likely to barely make it

into a 1965 "short stabs" poem

by Ted "bowl over" Berrigan

[*a tincture gives birth to a gravely verve*]

Barbara Kruger is enshrined in the window

of the Whitney's 1987 Biennial

[*a mixture is worth a thousand one-line serves*].

Nei

ther

speaking the unspeakable nor saying

the

unsayable

(though no doubt slurring

the unslurrable): never only

dedef

ining, always rec

onstricting (libidinal

flow just another

word for loose

st

ools). There was an old lady who lived in a

zoo,

she had so many admirers

she didn't know what to rue. Li

ke

a dull blade with a greasy handle (a

                docent page with an

   unfathomable ramble). Poetry's

like a spoon, with three or four

      exemptions: in effect only

off-peak, void

    were permitted by Lord,

   triple play

on all designated *ghost* phonemes

 (you mean morphemes)
[don't tell me what I mean!
].

    Rhymes may come and

rhymes may go, but ther

  e's

            no crime like presentiment. To refuse

               the

  affirmation

           of

(a)

                       straight-forward

     statement

(sentiment)

is

not

to

be

so

bent-over

with

irony

as

to

be

unable

to

assert

anything
but
to
find

such

statement

already

undermined

by the resistance

it

pretends

to

overpower

by

its

idealism

masked as

realism.

What? No approach

too gross if it gets a laugh. In Reagan's

vocabulary, freedom's

just another word for "watch out!" (I

pride myself on my pleonastic a[r]mour.)   {ardour}

(Besides.)

Love may come and love may

go

but uncertainty is here forever.
{profit?}

(There was an old lady

who lives in a stew…)

(A picture is worth 44.95 but no price can be
put on words.)

She can slip and she can slide, she's every

parent's j

oy & j

i

b

e

(guide)

.

In dreams begin a lot of bad
poetry.

Then where is my place?

Fatal Error F27: Disk directory full.

The things I

write are

not about me

though they

become me.

You look so bec

oming, she said, attending the flower pots.

I'm a very

becom

ing guy

(tell it to

)

. That is, better

to

become than
(gestalt f[r]iction)

{traction?}
{flirtation?}

to

be: ac

tuality

is just around

the corner (just a spark

in the dark); self-actualization a glance in

a tank of concave [concatenating] mirrors. Not

angles, just

tangles. From which

a direction emerges, p

urges. Hope

gives way

to tire tracks. On the

way without stipulating

the destination,

the better

to get there (somewhere,

other

).

THE MAGIC PHONEME FOR TODAY IS "KTH".

Funny, you don't look

gluish. Poetry: the show-

me business.

You've just said the magic phoneme!

"Don't give me

any of your

show-me business."

She wore blue velvet but I was color blind and insensible.

Heavy tolls, few

advances. Are you cl

os

e

to your m

other?

The brain of Bill Casey preserved in a glass jar deep under-
cover in Brunei.

Andy

        Warhol is the

           P. T. Barnum

of the
    (late)
  twentieth century

                             :

there's a

succor dead every twenty seconds.

A depository of suppositories

  (give it me where it counts:

        one and

        two and

         one

        two

         thr

                           eee)

.

    I had

it but

   I misp

laced

  it somewhere

         in the

   back burner

  of what

        is laug

hingly

  called m

y

  mind

            (my

  crim

      e). A

mind is a terrible thing to steal:

  intellectual property is also

  theft.

Ollie North, pound of chalk—but who is writing,

what is writing? Nor

all your regret change one word of it; yet so long as the blood flows in your veins there is ink

left in the bottle. FAKE A

WHISTLE TO WRITE (*spiritus sancti*). No "mere" readers only

writers who read, actors who inter-

act. Every day fades way, nor

all your piety

or greed bring back one hour: *take a swivel to*

strike.

(The near-heroic obstinacy of his refusal [inability?] to despair.)

   & who

     can say

   whether dejection or elation will

ensure the care for, care

        in

    the world that may lead us

weightless, into a new world or

      sink us, like lead

   baboons,

     deeper into this o

          ne? Yet

        you have to admit it's highly

drinkable.

Delish.

I imagine you unbespectacled, upright,

dictating with no hint of undercurrent,

a victim of the tide.

What if

success scares you so much that at the point of some

modest acceptance, midway through

life's burning, you blast out

onto the street, six-shooters smoking, still a rebel.

For what?

Of course new ventures always require risk, but by carefully

analyzing the situation, we became smart risk

takers. Fear of

softness characterized as rounded edges, indecisiveness, need to

please

versus the humorless rigidity of the "phallic"

edge, ready

to stand erect, take

sides (false dichotomy, all dichotomies).

An affirmation that dissolves into the fabric of

                unaccounted

desires, undertows of an imaginary that cannot be willed away but

                                neither need be mindlessly

        obeyed. *What's that?* If it's not

good news

        I don't want to hear it (

                        stand up and leer.) Our new

        service orientation

    mea

                                        nt

not only changing the way we wrote poems but also diversifying

into new poetry services. Poetic

        opportunities

,

        however, do not fall into your lap, at least not

very often. You've got to seek them out, and when you find them

                you've got to have the knowhow to take advantage

of them.

            Keeping up with the new aesthetic environment is an ongoing

process: you can't stand still. Besides, our current fees

        barely cover our expenses; any deviation from these levels

would

mean working for nothing. Poetry services provide cost savings

to readers, such

as avoiding hospitalizations (you're less likely

to get in an accident if you're home reading poems), minimizing

wasted time (*condensare*), and reducing

adverse idea interactions

(studies show higher levels of resistance to double-bind
political programming among those who read 7.7 poems or
more each week

).

Poets deserve compensation

for such services.

For readers unwilling to pay the price

we need to refuse to provide such

service as alliteration,
internal rhymes,
exogamic structure, and
unusual vocabulary.

Sharp edges which become shady groves,

mosaic walkways, emphatic asymptotes (asthmatic microtolls).

The hidden language of the Jews: self-reproach, laden with
ambivalence, not this or this either, seeing five sides to
every issue, the old *pilpul* song and dance, obfuscation

clowning as ingratiation, whose only motivation is never
offend, criticize only with a discountable barb: Genocide
is made of words like these, Pound laughing (with Nietzsche's
gay laughter) all the way to the canon's bank spewing forth
about the concrete value of gold, the "plain sense of the
word", a people rooted in the land they sow, and cashing
in on such verbal usury (language held hostage: year one
thousand nine hundred eighty seven).

There is no plain sense of the word,

nothing is straightforward,

description a lie behind a lie:

but truths can still be told.

These are the sounds of science (whoosh, blat,
flipahineyhoo), brought to
you by DuPont, a broadly diversified company dedicated to
exploitation through science and industry.

Take this harrow off

my chest, I don't feel it anymore

it's getting stark, too stark

to see, feel I'm barking at Hell's spores.

The new sentience.

As if Harvard Law School

was not a re-education camp.

I had decided to go back

to school after fifteen years in

community poetry because I felt

I did not know enough to navigate

through the rocky waters that

lie ahead for all of us in this field.

How had Homer done it, what might Milton

teach? Business training turned

out to be just what I most needed.

Most importantly, I learned that

for a business to be successful, it

needs to be different, to stand out

from the competition. In poetry,

this differentiation is best

achieved through the kind of form

we present.

Seduced by its own critique, the heady operative with twin
peaks and a nose for a brain, remodeled the envelope she
was pushing only to find there was nobody home and no
time when they were expected. Water in the brain,
telescopic Malthusian dumbwaiter, what time will the train
arrive?, I feel weird but then I'm on assignment, a plain blue
wrapper with the taps torn, sultan of my erogenous bull's
eyes, nothing gratis except the tall tales of the Mughali
terraces, decked like plates into the Orangerie's glacial
presentiment . . .

    No,

only that the distinction

between nature and

culture may obs

cure

the

b

odily

gumption of language.

Hello

my name is Max Gomez

(g

houlis

hness is it

s own rewa

rd).

(Commanding without being a command.)

Or else to say,

Catalogs are free, why not we?

Clear as f

udge.

Then what can I believe in?

(She'd rather exploit

than be exploi

ted.) If you break it, you

won't have it anymore.

Solemn in functional midrift, tooting at

bellicose grinding, who can no more bear witness to the doddering

demise of diplomacy than uproot the cancer at the throat of those

trajectories.

"Daddy, what did you

do to stop the war?"

[p-
=]ovwhiu2g97hgbcf67q6dvqujx67sf21g97b.c.9327b97b987b87j 7
7td7tq98gdukbhq g9tq9798 icxqyj2f1o8ytscxags62jc .<Mz[
-\ io

We may be all one body but we're sure as hell not one mind.

(Tell her I had to

change my plans.) It's not

what you

know but

who knows

about it

& who's

likely to

squeal

.   *Button*

your lip, cl

    asp your tie, you

,

    re on the B team. (A job

by any other name

would smell as

sour.) *It's*

                not an operating system it

,

      s an

op

     erating environm

      ent.

Besides

Sunsickness

Blame it on resembling, as if it would

change so easily, rough up glares

or trace avenues by fingertip.

You skirt on top afraid to sink

into and why not

falter, marched into elides, forked by

definition or conscripted from declamation—

the founding harbors faced it thus.

Then alone on hooks, trying

to get loss, the ground

refusing way. There's

no point, you proceed with intermittent

steps, & when the starting line appears

it can't be said

it's the same. No inanity suited

better than this poled tack. Nor

too much light either—heaving like

you'd just been hit in the face by a

wave—yet no particle

cares that much. I'd wager you've

had it by now—burn or defraud your

comeuppance as some sort of serial madness,

pegged to the flap that won't mind its

places. There was azure, agate, fool's

dust, but I never got any, just this

speculative bonfire. I'd give you credit

for that—but credit never satisfied

you. & after that there's only bone or blood

or sinew & not enough to share. Certain

things are private or anyway demand

privacy—but I'd be reluctant to say

who. No more than you I'm content

to lay low, tank up on decompression

& sing a chord or two—not possible

to remember many more than that. Or failing

to note the calm (calamity), fall prey to

remoter executions (I mean command

from distant quarters). There is a choir

here & don't know whether to blow

it out or blow it up. Less & less

to hold onto but more & more to do, be

done. If that doesn't stretch the point

too far. Going cold turkey or lukewarm

tongue. Not my language—just a lot of

luggage—but no use jettisoning the fading

with eau de cologne. Not my handle—

just a lot of tags on bags of baggage

that look

none too familiar. Then everybody

drops from sight & all the

wrong things said repeat themselves like

so many masquerades you can't pull

yourself out of. & screaming down

the hall without any signs of cause.

Pleading for hope when hope was just

the problem. Or should I throw a pie

in your face? (Pronoun slips on banana.)

—Michael writes of sun, but all I can think

of is sunsickness, too much in the sun

never a daughter. As if God's

light still shone on we who have shaded

our eyes. A few phrases remain,

but the drift is vanish. No way out

& no way in—a straight call to blast.

Adrift on stage for all to view—

the cringe, the sigh, the curvilinear

elide. The scholar-trancemaker hangs

from the end of a trope and asks

to be cut down. An umbilical cord

signifies no less. Yet despite, I can now see

or is it all

a mistake? & does it splatter?

The important thing is the sweep by which

the specific is hampered

on its way to the

laundry. The "only objective comment"

lifted from the interrogation, then fingered

in this historical fantasy some have undertaken

to get out of. & so our

Reviewer can state that his false assertions

are "absolutely true" & "patently true" even

in the face of being absolutely false &

patently misleading. *Facts are a dime a*

dozen but opinions are like pearls. Society's

sailed amid so many stuffed shirts. The road

redelivers the redaction. Yet form can contain

almost nothing, just enough. & bursts

onto the floor waving & jumping up &

down. Sleighbells of an anticipated foreclosure

chiming at a frequency beyond reach

yet driving to distraction all the

same; which is to say

without goal & undecidable

expectation—can't even say

toward—& naming the passage time or

placelessness. Getting in bed with promise

& waking up with make-believe.

Fortunately impecunious, at least on a

materials level. Floor board, window

pane, ceiling fan, . . . *Cold* as a cow

with a long tail going to confession, *crazy*

as a one-legged chair at an ass-kicking contest,

nervous as wet fog, *silly* as a bedbug

in a brass bra, *smelly* as a white man

on election day, *I* enters the canvas.

Then what would you know the meaning

of? Hard as honey, white as flint, loud

as the snow, dumb as mud . . . There

be another horizon, boots on bay, time

left for every day. It's not as if

it hasn't been said before or won't be

said another time, but never quite

the same. Soft as midnight, clear as

dead . . . With the radio you always

turn this sort of thing off & now you're

p(l)aying for it. Floating entirely

inside the dump, unmaking proportion

in small-mouthed widgets encapsulated

astride phantom departures. Slow &

sullen; fast & nasty. [Please do not turn

page until completion of song.] For which I

languish, in thousand lacerations entangled.

Demark wave, implosion of what

is vapor. Days stifling of cork &

circles of music, sordid front mounted, enlarged

trembling like spectre of corpses adorned

(absorbed). & the fissures

elevate themselves & grunt

& the savor forces its

effects. Like as to as & what to what remains.

Me won voice. Me other is:

An objection: haze of the subject

          brought to a locus.

An aberration: filter as creator—aspire

to what is dejectedly broken

occasionally the inflection of meteoric

          & terminal vagueness.

Everything marked, no need to fence.

Sopping hard & alike as

a fiddle & a dive. A simple no

that knows no answer. & *if he say* cut off their

hands, then he shall have his tongue cut out.

But revenge is for cues &

plates (tools &

states), defiance for the rest who wait

& are willing. For what

you may learn is that by going

down into the secrets of your

own crimes you descend

into the secrets of all

mimes (minds). Anyway:

some other. Worlds

hourly changing

sparring with cause to an

unknowable end. Asking

no less, demanding no

more.

Desalination

Then suddenly and without explanation
a bell rings. A grifter, his hands
covered by calfskin gloves, drives to
the station house to receive the goods.
Exemplary passages are cited. A
mystical blond with a scintillating
hat devours the nightlife. Overtures
are made to the underlying functionaries
in the hope that they might oil
the machinery. Fades prompt petty
tirades on the part of the tired
professor. Enabling fictions adorn
the prisoner's cells. In a minute
you can hear the dust settle on the
settee. The troupe fans out to
outflank the patrol. Portions
of lockets are auctioned at poolside.
A gazelle collides with a zebra

on the crowded skyway. Sentiment

cements the well-settled arrangement.

The fabricator eschews her prognostication.

Streetlamps crash into pounding

surf. Foreign lances punctuate the intermission.

A billiard pictures a tumbling

terrace. Sewage accumulates at rearmost

flexpoint. Plumage flutters from

above, gift of a departed origin.

The regulator consults the ordinance

but cannot determine its application.

Sustenance evaporates in subsequent

slumber. Amulets emit armatures.

An obligation meets its reward. Laundry

revolves in large metal tumblers filled

with soapy water. The radio covers

the burn in the table. Headwaiter

pockets tip from man in wool

suit, makes bet. Snow obliterates

the distinction between here & eternally.

Man's body stocking constricts the flow

of his blood. Oil tankers pour steam

into the gulf, upsetting the balance

of argument and insularity. Sorcery

threatens the petulant perpetuators.

Unequal in demand, frightening in

reward, flares appear dim

& the sky a tenement ceiling.

Unguents unnerve the future bookie's

wry predicament, mindful of deeds

left unfinished, duties not

discharged. Crumbling

into the Seine, memories of mysteries never

conceived. Then drops a lantern, a

picture window. Notation develops on top of

nuance. Crusts accrue like pillows

in a fight. Voiced as if regard were

trust or limousines malteds. The fun

is over before the fun begins. As when

a chance to speak becomes a chance to

slip: accommodation its own desperation, dispute

its own punishment. Pulling a dumbwaiter

& wishing for water. Discoloration of the enmazed
tractor parts—shifting through the pieces to find
the hearth. Hunt or hunched or clump or
confront. Roads roll into the harbor, with
no sign of the travelers. The crow flies
over the abandoned mine, irrespective of
penetratable homilies. Slow, maybe slender, taking
foreground for must. Craters cantilever to the corner.
A forager flushes his finds. Sacrifice
deploys secreted salvage. Burgers
bounce busily. Ratiocination cops
plea to lesser offense. Curls dwindle
in the high-pressure dome. The dreidel
begins to wobble wildly before tumbling to
ground. Emanations suffuse the body.
Sound permeates the *schul*. Young man
with horn can't hit imaginary note.
Steeplechase cascades through valley.
Someone says something. Motor oil materializes
miraculously. Camels stagger in the desert.
Snowballs batter the Mercedes as it speeds

through the puddle splashing the pedestrians.

The bride, tripping on trail, makes her way

to the launch. Holsters pile up in the checkroom.

The mission is cancelled. Balloon slips

from hand and floats into sky, like

the soul of Jesus meeting

its father. The bus disappears on route

to Jakarta. Holiday sales mask the despair

of a populace exhausted by good cheer and bad

chocolate. Ice coats the windows and railing

of the fabled outhouse. An apprentice disconnects

the hose that irrigates the pavilion's

ostentatious gardens. Workmen

erect the towering edifice according to plan, then

report to next job.

Locks Without Doors

I.

Will you promise not to get mad

    if I tell you something? Nothing

              notable except the prism without

     light effects. Except that

        expectations stymie hunger for

 exceptions, such that

     dedication rumples the doily

   while in a tugboat there's

too little chance for remorse.

       Like pillars of sand at a Revivalist

            Meeting or pockets of pumice at a

 Pita Party. For when the fire chief

          told Pickles that he could stay

  the cat knew he had finally

    found a home. Any other solution

    would be shallow and unseemly and so

seemingly inconsolable. An

    inexorable

        float bombarding an quixotic emission,

 a fleeting factotum culminating in

gesellschaft.

        Settle for less

and you'll get less.

    A kettle of fish

is worth two pints of pink chocolate, a

    bucket of kool-aid twice a coterie of

        covens.

Slump not lest slip, slumber, swagger into

indelicacy, delirious indolence. The

    world is half right, half flight, half

sorrow, half sliced. The

        eucalyptus

bloomed in the decor, the dooryard

    extruded the stall.

2.

For long have I entombed my love
Less fleck than flayed upon
Who quaint and wary worry swarms
In tides lament nor laminations ore
As stare compares a bellys tumble
Have I awaited by the slope
Of lumined ledgers lumbering links
Foregone though never bent

3.

Not that I mean to startle just
unsettle. The settlers pitched their tents
into foreign ground. All ground is
foreign ground when you get to know
it as well as I do. Well I wouldn't agree.
No agreement like egregious
refusal to hypostatize a suspension.
Suspension bridges like so many
drummers at bat, swatting flies in
the hot Carolina sun. No, son, it
wasn't like that — we only learned we
had to be proud not what's worth taking
pride in.

4.

Looking for truth but finding only
memory

5.

Like two boats with one oar
Two lives with one core

6.

Forest ranger, inflatable stranger
Show me the place to flop down
Longing to go, got a beer & hoe
Deep under this frown

My daddy told me
Were certain men
Sell you for fodder
In ocean of sense
Tried to talk to you
Given my word
No sense talking
To men with no curves

7.

I can't but make it con-
fluesce.

8.

never knew what west is / best is

9.

I got
no eyes

all ears
tear verbs

for very long
had no song

give me a day
to make my sway

glow and rasp
will not last

be kind
slow mind

go blow
fill holes

come clean
go away

in summer
get butter

floor plan
poor slant

regularize
close your eyes

summary
mummery

grumble
fumble

ice cold
innuendoes

in it
for keeps

all right
too slight

mike knows
it's over

sam helps those
cooperate

10.

not for you
the hullabaloo

11.

No touch like your touch
 Tiled to the flap it spun
Holding windows make-shift blouse
 In rolling tide would crest

Cold lurch spills spit fold
 Wild by such splat is come
Flushing sinews buttressed blast
 On twirling slides next bounce

12.

I'll swallow my pride
 Before I die
I'd bury my song
 Without your arm

13.

The quality of Hershey's is not
too great although I always preferred
Skippy's smooth to crunch. If
Devil Dogs are not so good as Mars
bars, Camel's can still do what
no Virginia Slim dares. There was a time
I'd take a chance on generic
but I've learned to take pride in Tide.

14.

"Put em away
or else I'll
take them away"

"I'll smack you on the face you say that again"

"There go
the lassoes"

15.

lovely to see you
lolling about the lake
eating cake

16.

the brotherhood of sleeping cars

17.

I used to be Detroit
Now I'm Tennessee
I used to be distraught
Now I'm hard to get along with

Then again the quality of Jersey is not
much to wriggle your teeth about
five o'clock I'd say
nothing about it to him at all
you've meant to her & she
turned it over in her head
straight for the moors

18.

you got a license for that torque?

19.

Books can be deceiving, for instance
that look you gave me does not faze me
or it'll be a frozen fog in Alberta
before the slot delivers.

20.

"He stepped right on our castle"

"It's a real crab with flaws"

"Don't blame me I'm from Idaho"

"Don't blush it only appears to be happening"

21.

Put lack in your pipe and stroke it.

22.

Not the hand
in the glove
but the mitten
in your mouth.

How I Painted Certain of My Pictures

"You say I'm like a Jewish mother but the kid
is losing weight." Turning by turns as though
turns would make it different. Sunny
with shallows all about, the solvent
flush of fiduciary abandon. Mayhem
that may be all right for Craig or
Thomas but makes Dora duller. *By crater
lake, the minds too late.* Or do the
pushed pins pullulate; not that
the motivation to continue could ever be
just go on. Ingratiatingly grouchy, guardedly
unconscious. Or else the pride of admission
is not worth spitting on. *I got to
gargle* but the loop's on the V C R
& the pillow's in deep
fry. Similar
to dusting for fiberboard after each

feel. "I

don't like mistakes, but purposes

truly scare me." The lorry has left the

levy lest the sandwiches lay

lost, looted.

Which cries out suddenly, incorrigibly

that the gasket's blown an apricot. Or

there'll be no more glowing. As in

a deed is worth only half a word, over

three-foot bird (seldom

blurred). & then

the launches sway in the cringe, fix

flutters against green & yellow

mutters (mothers). "Thomas

is in my place & won't

move." But it's not birds

that are the problem. As if the

ordinary

were just there answering

our call but we

won't sound it

out, or find the work

too demanding (de-

meaning), too extra

ordinary. There

are sleigh bells I know but never

mine. Yet nothing I've lost, nothing

yet to

find. If that makes you sad

then I'm sad too, even though we've

never met or meet just now. Events

are no protection from circumstance

& circumstance is a positive hindrance.

  Darling girl, darling boy
  Let's burn the house
  Tear down the ploys

Stalled among the pantomimes,

obsolete rimes. Never saw a bird

that didn't want to fly—but there must be

pigeons of different feather. Yet woman & man

are no feather at all. Crazy like this

rag gun rapping on my brain's floor.

So skip to the slaughter
Just like you ought'er
& take that smirk off your grimace

Yet kindness has such a bad

name, deliverance no less. Trees won't

say it any better than "O!"

rings. Every syllable stings. & that's the

hardest thing to stomach on a low-noise

diet, if you can sink your teeth into

the

thought that all that sound gotta be

digested. Anemic

poetry—or roughage?—for the health-

continent society? But

why prize distraction over direction, song over

solemnity? The times detail a change of

pockets & everybody's loopy, mind made

up with hospital corners, while the leaves

of our lives unsettle their occupation. Or

is it a value simply to glide in the

turbulent air & push back when things

get foreshortened? The fate of the earth—

like if the world doesn't care who will?

"Don't scream so close my face!"

That we have to inhabit the world to know where

the earth might be, *is*. Then where was

it (was it?) lost. When I get

home I'll glue it together as a little book.

& if that won't work we can play Billie-

come-gravely all the way to the moon. *If*

the clue slips tear it. Nor jingle your

jaundiced gestures in my directions.

I'm as plump as a cherry on the tree

George Washington never chopped, as carefree

as a hornet in amphetamine

dive. You'll

be lucky if you get out of here with your

yarmulke intact—but the shadow world will

intervene before the last lost moment. "People

don't like you because you're a brat—selfish

& whiny." Although if you brush your teeth

twice you'll get more than enough advice.

"I had to leave the job because I couldn't

stand the people & the work was totally

absorbing." Because humble is not

the same as

humiliated.

Notice which bugs.

& over & over again

with aesthetic turpitude

(Let's trade flavors).

Normally I'd say there was no jettisoning.

But my friend Frisby-Love took all she could take

before dead-ending in the herbervescent poker

patch. Darn this dated elan, these holes

of pure cheesecloth. *As if outside*

were anywheres at all. Bruised to the knees

in amours & cleaves. Confidence

just a prick—the man

on the barge selling

you the bridge between this thought

&

this.

Still waters run about as deep

as you can blow them. But it's time

I came clean & you swept the boat

(I mean cameo): floor-length conscription

with matching five-piece hush-orange ensemble.

Reading the riot act in the middle of

sacral pacts. "Whatever you say,

Sheriff!" "It's been a long day,

they always are." "But why can't I

go out because I can see children

playing?" Fluent in dreams, inconsolable

otherwise. "I guess I have you

to thank

for the mustard." I guess

we all just

want to go home to bed.

I guess

light doesn't even notice

it's going so fast.

Drum beats on the meridian, sun beats on the

Mercedes. Mr. Bush stares blankly

on the podium wondering what to do next. M.

Mitterand has some warm words for Danton. Mrs.

Thatcher bangs a few notes on her bagpipe.

The silencers click onto

the muzzles.

"I just don't want

to have to

go through that again."

I'll

just put down my

pen.

Exeunt.

Curtain.

ACTION!

The View from Nowhere

"Zip it up—I don't care—you listen

to me." Proscriptive or prescriptive: the weight

of tradition or

a tradition of weights. Just

waiting to get the go ahead from my friends on

the force. Blanked

out on parry when route

has found alternative to clown-out, suction. Running

to meter the lawn in consequence of which

showers departure. "Chill

off!" Confining

masquerade

to detail, touching

promise until you've fingered

the figures out of it, out of

yourself. &

yelling behind the truck, inaudible

to the exhaust,

like some nasty duck pounding against a pond.

The view I am going to suggest, I hope in

less obscure

language, is related to this.

Essentially, there are three

types of problems. Sometimes

with hardly a notion that she has

heard a word. Blue & blue-

black. For what's the point of having

different words if they mean the same

thing? Something made me

want to get out of the house. I

couldn't understand that money was going

to be burned

when people was

in need. But the issue

is different if we return

to the question posed at the beginning. In

addition to the question of objectivity is

the question of

scale. The importance of this

point will emerge when we see how complex

a psychological interchange constitutes

the natural development of sexual

abstraction. I felt

bad. I

felt cold. I felt

completely out of

it.

The article

paints a picture

of its author as seething with jealousy

& egomania—hopelessly out

of touch

with the material

that is his

putative

subject. The thing then to watch the spectacle

without being sucked up

in

it—for there is

a danger in finding yourself dictating

defenses to crimes not only not committed

but really just the opposite

of crimes—what

is left to be done. Of course, what

many have regarded as a liberating

permission

to write in otherwise unsanctioned ways

will provoke professional sanction-takers to see

only red. Because

of casuistical problems

like this

I prefer to stay with the original

unanalyzed distinction between what

one does to people

& what merely

happens to them as a result of what one

does. Notions

for a September day, lying in the

hay

of tumultuous enfolding.

All this

is as clear as day

right now. The crow

slides low over the abandoned

mine, looking for correspondence &

twine. While in Gaza

the rioters have

nothing

to lose

but loss.

The view I am

going

to suggest

I hope in less obscure language

is related to

this.

Virtual Reality

for Susan

Swear
  there is a sombrero
of illicit
    desquamation
(composition).

    I forgot to
 get the
    potatoes but the lakehouse
  (ladle)
    is spent
  asunder. Gorgeous
   gullibility—
or,
    the origin
    of testiness
(testimony).

Laura
 does the laundry, Larry
lifts lacunas.
    Such that
details commission of
    misjudgment over 30-day
intervals.

              By
the sleeve is the
    cuff & cuff
link (lullaby, left offensive,
    houseboat).

Nor
  let your unconscious
 get the better of you.
    Still, all ropes
 lead somewhere, all falls
  cut to fade.
I.e.: 4 should always be followed
  by 6, 6 by 13.

 Or if
  individuality is a false
front, group solidarity is a
 false fort.

"ANY MORE FUSSING & YOU'LL
  GO RIGHT TO YOUR ROOM!"

She flutes that slurp
admiringlier.

   Any more blustering & I
  collapse as deciduous
    replenishment.

 So sway the
swivels, corpusculate the
 dilatations.
  For I've
 learned that relations
  are a small
twig in the blizzard
   of projections
 & expectations.
  The story
 not capacity but care—
    not size but desire.

      & despair
makes dolts of any persons, shimmering
in the quiescence of
longing, skimming
      disappointment & mixing it
with

      breeze.

          The sting of
      recognition triggers
      the memory & try to
      take that apart (put
      that together).

          Popeye
no longer sails, but Betty
        Boop will always
     sing sweetlier
     sweetliest
than the crow who fly
      against the blank
  remorse of castles made
    by dusk, dissolved in
         day's baked light.

Emotions of Normal People

.

With high expectations, you plug

Into your board & power up. The

Odds are shifted heavily in your

Favor as your logic simulator comes

On-screen. If there's a problem

You see exactly where it's located

& can probe either inside or

Outside with a schematic editor.

English-like commands make

Communication easy. Auto-scale

Gets waveform capacity on-board

Without the need for monolithic or

Highpass switch debouncers &

Dissipation separators. For

Correlating interactions, the 16-

Bit data bus & interrupt controller

Lets you place a timestamp value on

Every transaction stored—at no

Cost to your memory depth.

Normalization then corrects for

Reflections & imperfections caused

By connectors & cables. Enter the

Digitalizing oscilloscope with 20

GHz bandwidth, 10 ps resolution, &

Floating-point primitives upwardly

Compatible with target-embedded

Resident assemblers & wet-wet

Compilers. & the fact that you can

Configure it yourself means you

Get exactly what you want—& cut

Down on chances for device failure.

Moreover, all systems components

Are easy to install & reconfigure

Since interconnections use a

Floating interface that produces

Consistent low-loss mating. Add

Real-time, transparent emulation

Capabilities, & the largest overlay

Capability in the industry, in a

Rugged package with state-of-the-

Art flash-converter overflow flags

& a family of workstations &

Servers that thrive in a multi-

Vendor environment. At which point

You can connect a bi-directional

Buffer or dumb terminal to the

Module's digital inputs & relay

Outputs with crystal-controlled

External trigger for jitter-free

Duplex data compression & protocol

Source codes.

Dear Fran & Don,

Thanks so much for
dinner last night. You two
are terrific—we knew that about
you, Fran, but, Don—we don't
meet rocket engineers such as
yourself very often and so
meeting you was a special treat!

>   Next time—our little
>   Italian restaurant!
>
>   Warm Regards,
>
>   Scott & Linda

Suddenly, in spite of
worrisome statistics that had unnerved
the Street, we
developed conviction and acted on it. Aside
from the arbs
and the rumor mill, the major trend remains up regardless of
street noise.
The liquidity is there, so any catalyst
should hasten the major direction. The market's internal tech-
nical condition is far from
overbought, which leaves
room to rally back to October's
2500.

I think our big problem is inhibiting post-normalization.

Success demands getting more from available space, taking
efficiency to extremes, paying less for improved performance.
Moreover, 2440 sacrifices none of 2430A's performance.

Intuitive user interfaces provide only part of the road map
out of the dark ages.

We've made debugging easier with differential nonlinearity,
monolithic time-delay generators, and remote-error sensing
terminals (RESTS). Yet, we still face a severe memory short-
age and rather than resolve the problem we're buying our way
out of it. We need a tariff on cheap foreign-made memory so
we can regroup our own. The current controversy, however,

stems from the attempts of several vendors to control the mar-
ketplace by promoting standards that especially benefit their
computing architecture.

I'd like you to meet Jane Franham.
Jane was my mother-in-law until I married
Jim. While I was sure of Joan's
love, I still
worried that she might be tempted
by other men. Now both hands
are able to work, since the magnifier
is suspended around
the neck on an adjustable length of
cord. We had argued about his
job before, about how wrong it was for a man with three kids
to spend so few days a year
at home, with
no end in sight. I
suspect that your father had an adrenal
gland tumor that was
driving his blood pressure
up. Lillie was very emphatic that she
wanted to be a ballet dancer; the nun thing
was just a passing
phase that lots of girls
go through. Lipstick
is meant to be the perfect
finishing touch—one that doesn't
compete with
your eyeshadow or clash
with your blushes.
Only
when the soup course
is finished is
the service plate
taken out. —*Who's the woman* YOU

most admire? Is it
Shirley Temple Black, Raisa Gorbachev, Phyllis
Schlafly, Winnie Mandela, Mother Teresa of
Calcutta, or Ella Fitzgerald?
After my neck surgery, Marge asked me
if I would be
investing in a lot of scarves.
The Cowley's
one exceptional
expenditure is the $583 they give every month
to their church.
This outlay represents nearly
15 percent of their budget. And
in 1985 and 1986, when the church was being enlarged
to include a 2,500-seat chapel, Dick and Carol
contributed nearly 25 percent
of their income. "The church is the focus
of our lives," says Carol.
She is a volunteer in the church
library; Dick teaches
adult Sunday school, accompanies the choir (on
trumpet), and
every Tuesday evening goes out on
"visitations".
However you come to terms
with your feelings about your husband, you must
face the fact that your son is totally
innocent of any
responsibility. No matter how much bitterness
his father deserves, you must not transfer it
to the boy. Define
brows with
brown eye-shadow
pencil; blend with
stiff brow brush
for natural
effect. Use

powder one shade darker
than skin tone. Brush on
temples
and under chin to widen
face. For long-lasting
color, dust lips
with translucent powder
before applying
lip
color. All
things considered
Joe
was a thoughtful
husband.
The
only thing nicer
than a letter from a friend
is taking the time to read it
over a warm cup of Orange
Cappucino.

In InteliCorp's KEE, frames are called units, properties of
units are called slots, and properties of slots are called facets.
In Teknowledge's 5.2, however, frames are called classes, prop-
erties of classes are called attributes, and properties of at-
tributes are called slots.

"When someone hits the board with the head in
That fashion, you can get a scalping eff-
Ect," Panzano said. "The board hits the head
And the skin is peeled back and it requires
Extensive suturing. The worst thing a
Diver can do is hit the board or the
Tower. When I see something like that, I
Get a sick feeling in my stomach."

If you would love to be living your life in a different way but don't want to spend a lifetime learning how . . . Dynamic short-term social therapy can empower you to make the moves you've been afraid—or unable—to make, in your personal life and your career. You don't have to be a victim of loneliness, depression, "mid-life crisis", indecisiveness, or regrets. Free up your ability to grow and change as you learn the emotional and social skills you need to be intimate and passionate. Write The Dysraphism Center for more information.

Bernstein's argument is an important one and his discussion is consistently thoughtful, energetic, and smoothly handled. Any reader of the modern verse epic will find *The Tale of the Tribe: Ezra Pound and the Modern Verse Epic* stimulating and provocative.

> *This hereby serves as your second*
> *and final return notice. Since our*
> *previous notice to you remained unanswered,*
> *we must assume you do not*
> *want your Casio 300 rear projection*
> *color TV or your three piece*
> *Cardin designer luggage. As previously detailed,*
> *this sophisticated color projection television viewing*
> *system features the latest in television*
> *technology. This set delivers rich contrast*
> *and sharp resolution. This system must*
> *be given away in order to*
> *comply with state and federal regulations.*
> *The same is true of the*
> *designer luggage by Pierre Cardin. Your*
> *failure to respond immediately will release*
> *your television to other persons located*
> *in your region. Please call 1-800-233-4797*
> *to schedule your tour of Tree*
> *Tops Resort. Operators are on duty.*

Which best describes your dress size? What brands of bar soap have been used in your household in the past 6 months? Which of the following hypoallergenic products are currently being used in your household? Which of the following best describes the sensitivity of your skin? To which of the following products have you experienced a negative reaction? On average, how many days per week do you use foundation? Do you use a facial cleanser *other than bar soap*? Do you or anyone in your family wear support pantyhose? What brands of underwear do you wear? How often have you used a nasal spray in the last 6 months? How many tablets of pain relievers are used in your household each month? Did you ever use a nonprescription pain reliever in capsule form? Do you own an automatic dishwasher? If so, how many loads do you do in your automatic dishwasher in an average week? Do you use Mexican sauces such as salsa or picante? If you have burned artificial firelogs in your fireplace, which brands do you burn most often? If anyone in your family practices heart attack prevention, how? Which of the following home improvements do you plan in the next 6 to 12 months? How many times did you medicate for diarrhea in the past year? Are you concerned about the side effects allergy medicine can cause (drowsiness, dizziness, insomnia, sleeplessness, dry mouth)? In an average month, how many calls are made by you and any other household member living with you to places outside your area code? Have you moved in the last year and during which month? How many vehicles are owned by members of your household? How do you feel about your present auto insurance company? Do you invest in or would you welcome literature describing special offers on securities? Which of the following do you own or have, or are you considering for first-time purchase or replacement within the next six months? What organizations do any members of your household belong to? How many times have you shopped by mail in the past month? Do you frequently donate by mail to any of the following?

Dear Mr. Chinitz:

I am writing to follow-up on two previous phone calls on this subject and because I will not be able to reach you by phone late this afternoon when you are scheduled to be in your office.

As you know, I called you on September 30 and October 2 to report a very loud vibrating noise coming from the main water risers in our apartment—a noise that affects the whole "R" line and can be heard in the hallway of the building. This noise persisted throughout the middle-of-the-night and into the day on the occasions I called. The noise was such as to prevent sleeping and thus is a disturbing and serious problem. Almando the super checked out every apartment on the rear line of 464 on October 2 while the noise was going on and found it appeared to be unrelated to any water use in those apartments.

Subsequent to that time, the situation had improved: the noise would occur sporadically for periods of five minutes to one hour. During the day today, however, the noise has been persistent from 11:00 am on. Typically, the vibration occurs for about 10 seconds and then stops for about 20 seconds. The hot water riser can be felt to shake: and the adjacent walls also shake.

I had hope that this situation had been resolved, but evidently not. Your urgent attention to this matter is necessary and would be most appreciated.

A 1985 survey shows that 23.3 percent of all writers write poetry—that's 2,180,000 people who are writing poetry and want to get published. *1989 Poet's Market* contains current, accurate, and complete information to help poets to do just that.

Poets will find out where and how to publish their poetry through 1,700 listings (550 of which are brand new) of mass circulation and literary magazines, trade book publishers, small presses, and university quarterlies. Updated listings

enable poets to accurately target their work to receptive
publishers. Poets will find details on who to contact, how to
submit work, types of poetry needed, comments from
editors, poets published, whether the publisher accepts
unsolicited poems, type of compensation (where appli-
cable), and sample lines of recently published poems. In
addition, each listing is coded according to the level of
submissions desired (beginner, experienced, or specialized).

Through 12 "Close-Up" interviews with such poets as
Richard Wilbur, 1987 Poet Laureate of the United States,
and Rita Dove, winner of the 1987 Pulitzer Prize for poetry,
poets will gain further insight into the process of writing and
publishing poetry. They'll also find advice on increasing their
chances of being published by knowing how to judge their
own work; participating in workshops, clubs, and network-
ing; working with regional publications; plus opportunities in
greeting card, poster, and postcard markets and information
on contests and awards.

**How do statesmen become aware of unfavorable shifts in
relative power and how do they seek to respond to them?
Who makes constitutional laws? Were early Americans a
distinctly modern people, a people without a past? This is
an exemplary work of mutually supportive normative
argument and empirical investigation. Reading it is like
backpacking through the nation's forests in company with
a modern-day Thoreau. Secondly, the posture that the
work takes is frankly quite liberal, and, in recent years,
open and undisguised liberalism has become something of
a debased currency. After absorbing these revelations and
analysis, it is hard to imagine comprehending the origins
and evolution of the cold war without them. Drawing on
the work of Indian and Japanese patients and displaying a
professional anthropologist's eye for telling detail, here is
the first comprehensive study of Protestant theological
concerns. A fascinating history that should be required
reading for any serious student of turn-of-the-century**

French gaiety. Abounds in rich description and valuable insight. Destined to become the definitive treatment for decades. All Americans who care about their country's place in the world will find this book worth reading.

Are you a normal person?

Probably for the most part you are.

Your sex complexes, your fears and furies and petty jealousies,

your hatreds and deceptiveness, only serve

to secure your normalcy. I can still remember

vividly the fear I once experienced, as a child,

when threatened, on the way to school,

by a half-witted boy with an air-gun.

But a person who calls himself

a psychologist is in a peculiar position

these days. Dr. Cuit P.

Tichter of the Johns Hopkins University

found that Norway rats

died quickly if their whiskers were clipped

and they were put into a

tank of water. Actually,

we have two emotional levels, one

fundamental and the other more or less

superficial. Actually,

most people need only a few close

friends, with a larger circle

of casual friends. Experiments show that

if someone says these

things to a man on his way to the office,

sometimes he can scarcely work

and will go home to bed. Besides,

being busy is

not a virtue in itself!

There are no adequate emotional outlets

for many stresses and people who depend completely

on their emotions frequently find themselves

in jail. This explains why

persons with father-in-law, familial

or boss troubles develop

painful spasms. The intestine is

as sensitive to bombardments

from the brain as the skin of some people

to sun rays. The

bowel is a bear for punishment.

In such an atmosphere

a husband can develop a disturbing

sense of inferiority. He begins

to doubt that he still has the capacity

to be attractive. He may

become so convinced that he has lost his

charm that he no longer

makes any effort to look nice or

appear charming. Of course, the

opposite type of upbringing can be just as

harmful. Of course,

you can't grade husbands like apples or oranges,

dropping each

through a slot previously evaluated for size,

shape, dis-

position, and domesticity.

"Men like to be bossed," says Dr.

Cleo Dausson, University of Kentucky

psychologist and authority on

masculinity. "Men are fearful. Glandular

differences make them five times more fearful

than women. They attach more

importance to security than women do. Emotionally

they are never

on the same keel two days in a row; as a result, they need

constant reassurance." But some parents

always act fearsome and

protective toward their children, not thinking

that by killing

their nerve they are also killing their chances

of having rich,

exciting, and successful lives. Children

are born with

practically no fears and if not repressed

by their overanxious and tyrannical

parents

would have a natural courage that would

sustain them throughout life. Nor can I second

your notion that

you've got moral grounds for divorce. Rather, I think

your

misery calls for psychiatric treatment. In other words, the

mother's natural reflex equilibrium

could not be restored to a

completely resting or balanced condition until Teddy

had learned

to perform his part of the rug-folding

process perfectly, and was

further able to take the initiative

in directing his mother's

movements so that they would cooperate completely

with his own. Again the explanation

of their incompetence in passing a mental

test may lie in the subjects' seeming

inability

to regard fellow students as rivals, or to feel

any element of

opposition

in either the test itself or the examiner. They

frequently appear just as well satisfied

with a poor record as a

good one and seem

willing to submit to

any degree of hardness or

criticism or reproof from the teacher

or examiner without

assuming the least antagonism

of attitude.

In any case, sarcasm

is evidence of a sadistic trend in one's

personality.

Debris of Shock / Shock of Debris

The debt that pataphysics owes to sophism

cannot be overstated. A missionary with a horse

gets saddlesores as easily as a politburo

functionary. But this makes a mishmash of overriding ethical

impasses. If the liar

is a Cretan I wouldn't trust him

anyway—extenuating contexts wouldn't amount

to a hill of worms so far as I

would have been deeply concerned about

the fate of their, yes, spools. Never

burglarize a house with a standing army,

nor take the garbage to an unauthorized

junket. Yet when I told the learned

ecologist about my concern for landscape

she stared unsympathetically into the

carbon. Mr. Spoons shook his head, garbled his

hypostases. To level with you we'd have

to be on the same

level. Then, with all honesty, we can

only proceed to deplane. Looking for society

in a lamppost will not necessarily eliminate

need for empirical

evidence. There are the

below-the-surface conduits

to consider. As a rule, I keep

my mittens in the drawer. Structure

is metaphorical, function metonymic. Meaning

my aim is to blur

the distinction between logic and normalization.

("Though I still don't get how confusion

is supposed to be positive?") Are they literally

bricks or are they literal steps? The infernal

machinery of missing harness, by the bus,

gates close to malediction, as in

get off my bunt, churning

in make-work flirtation, shocked to find a bandit

loosened . . . Venetian red (Rem), prussian

ultramarine (Rem), shiva red, thick

red, thick pink, thick ochre, medium green

paintstick (thick), thin black, thin

ochre, thin

red, paper palette, tissues, garbage bags,

wax.

Yet it is the virile voice of authority, the condescending

smugness in tone, that is thrilling. What

does it matter that he hasn't any . . . "Creative

goals and financial goals are identical: we just

have different approaches on how to research

those goals, and we have different definitions

of risk." A localization that may not

dovetail with forced archaization, which

is the groundswell of our importunity. &

speaking of "pressmen's licence", here is a truly

novel instance of "creating facts"

riddled with holes like baloney. *Respond:*

yes or no. The point not to right wrong

but to come to terms

with error. It's not only

the wrong road but the wrong

destination; still if

there's no way back, there's company

in the

loss. Heeding without ceding . . . Couples

dancing in the snow, in the blinding

light. No matter how much you protest.

"If I'd have lived longer, I'd have lost

even more money." For months he retreated

into his inner sanctuary, emerging only for meals

& sleep; once, stealing through its

locked doors, we briefly glimpsed

the spot: bare

walls without furniture or implement, floor

covered with thick black

loam. Better

a barber than a splendor

be. Fool's

gold

is the only kind of gold I

ever cared about.

The men, having lost their comrades in the

explosion, returned the next day to the mine

& the memory: what other

image of courage could have

so little capital & so much

weight? The salt

of the earth is the tears

of God, torn for

penitence at having created this plenitude

of sufferance. So we dismember (disremember)

in homage to our maker, foraging

in fits, forgiving in

forests, spearing what we take

to be our sustenance: belittling to rein things

in to human scale. A holy land parched

with grief & dulled

envy. The land is soil

& will not stain; such

hope as we may rise from.

Heart in My Eye

Motion rises, sustains a
predilection in askance
who periodize location, slush

boat to chimes
slows emotion, like as
in thumping pummels
or pulverizes punt

vicarious want to
be possessed no room
arrays diphthong slope

gumption gum drilled or
guttered, the contraption
is delinquent must fly
trap or elevate

theatrical equivalent of lozenge
a.k.a. e'er do-well seamster
stirs up corollary antidote

or weightlier osmosis
stems looking glass affect
coddling codices in
endoskeletal humor mongering—you'd

have to admit—
belies the unpoetic poetic
who cruises palatially—

all adrift intended—I'll
get slumpy and
maybe open a garden
(leveled at about

30,000 fleet)—or hate
the boom-shebang effect
fostered at time

interlock, station flayed by
inoperable hampers, obsequious
swoops, as pulp bumps
plop, thingamawhoseit buffle

joint, glassed in gradually
gestures of gerrymand
origin, jitters jocose oblong—

nor say this—
materials not hard to
locate but reform—
like like or as

before, getting a
taxi in a sandstorm
breathes (not breaths)

a lie of belief
tokes of congregation
voids convivial handtray intubation
until detains corrode

lavalier pistol-whip upholstery
larvae of dysfunction
branding witless hip, demarcation

baloney, scintillating sway
of deadbeat ejaculation, sipping-
good aluminum: anything
that can be forgot

will be forgotten
blue ashtray on a
plexiglass puncture, plowed

to enclosure, moment before
enunciation: *I left*
you there but you
have never found

me though I hide
in visibility and
wade higglety pigglety among

archways or ski lifts
courting caresses while plummeting
occasionally to shoreline
sighting concavities like the

mannequin that had
no manners, trading flops
for angular inebriation

(awful salvage), lighting delay
as if details
could reverse the course
of reason's palsy:

heart in my eye
remorse buckles under
weight that overpowers all

I call mine
all touched by such
exposure imagination flings
tools formed in shell-

bent plan we
mourn at singular unleavening
excretes by fold

Reveal Codes

It is often said that the bladder is an unreliable
witness. I've felt that way myself coming back
from a sluggishly encumbered day at the computer
bank. "They clammed up like so many turtles
in overdrive"—but only if you didn't get to know
their Mercurial propulsions. There's a version
that says quell the branches before you braid
or at least unload the interfusing hot buttons. Don't
know much about chopped wax either, loop
the reliquary, some cross-valent comet coming at
50,000 kilobytes per minute per mention, I left
the rack at the store but recalled the combination
to the cross, "he would suck up to
an octopus if he thought it would strangle somebody
for him", no pork barrel just juiced petunias . . .

It was one of those almost unfamiliar
sections of LA, just beyond the tar
pits, where you could get steak
& eggs for breakfast for under ten
& change. I wasn't
quite a regular but they knew me well enough
to bring the order without asking
too many questions. It was
a dive I went to to get my mind off work, my attention
Intermittent Diffuse
with just enough juice
to register the scene at the end table
by the picture of Hydra.

Ripping through the water like it was so much
Swiss cheese

"The only thing Swiss about you is the baloney!"

Dear Mr. Charles,

I wish and pray this letter finds you
in the best of health and cheers. May I
introduce myself as a missionary priest
working for North East India with its
thousands of dowtrodden people, suffering
from the pangs of poverty, illiteracy
diseases, etc. Hence in their name this
begging letter to you for any little help.

So many innocent and poor children
are to be fed, educated, and looked
after. Timely aids for emergency needs
give us tensions in distress we
have no other way than to make
appeal in folded hands to kind
hearted people.
                    Fr. Pallatty M.
                    Madras 600 008

Dried ice or crunched innuendo, on your toes then on your
knees. To capitalize Despair—that was the old way; to
capitalize on despair, who promises an aspiring future
in piece goods . . . The boat found the hay but the ocean
had turned to a symphony of suction. *So long sweet tuna,
so long gefilte fish.* The only true traditions
the ones we invent to vent the spleen of the inconsolable
loss of history's ambient diffusion and victory's
unsparing parry. Witless in the rain, sober
in the dew . . .

Or more due than ever done, when debts
Soak the morning and regrets eventide

>My name is Necromancer
>My sister calls me Still
>I'm widely known as Cast Away
>'ve trouble with my Trill

Yet despite the disintegration of his personality, the
foolishness of his actions, his excessive drunkenness
and incurable extravagance, Goldsmith was, and is,
a great man—a man of rare talents that border on
genius, one of the finest natural writers in the English
language.

For Blake's art is ornamental
& rhetorical, not organic &
formal.

Slip & slide
pop 'n' fizz
blink and whine
drop, spin

There hangs the fade, there the woolen shoes.
The roof has swoops—
two fools under one hood, alarmed to the teeth
one with an eye on the sail
other with ear to the—.

Where the carcass is, there
the crow flies.

Swarming around the bandshell
waiting for the buzz saw
or Buick Pompadour convertible

coupe or any so-called doze-proof
buffet

Or, to put it more bluntly, no gain
no pain. As if no pain wasn't
pain enough.

This buttons the cue when the overlay
is toggled. "Hot keys"—i.e.
combinations you press to access
a resident, or underlying, program, as
"control" and "home", "mother" and "blanket",
"disguise" and "revenge".

As in a lifeguard's better than
no guard. As if
you could guard life
without blanking it out.

My friend Polly Vocal called the other
day just to say hello. I decided not
to pick up and returned the call
to the machine on her other number.

Go On Get Down

"Do they have a bar here?"

Short stabs or quick hits or is there
an exit & is it near the "exit" sign?

Is the Pope Polish? Does $3 + 5$ equal $5 + 3$?
Is Lincoln buried in Grant's Tomb? Is
the South Bronx a WASP enclave? Will this
burn at Fahrenheit 451? Is Napoleon the President
of the Bahamas? Is Communism finished? Do

hearts break when you don't touch them?
Are the rich getting richer or are you just
glad to see me?

"I didn't give it to you with any sand so
why do you give it to me with sand?"

"Well, Blanche, I just brought the egg over here
because the recipe says to separate two eggs."

LET'S CALL THE POLICE!

"Let's call the Swedish delegation!"

Call me irresistible or call me unreliable
but don't call me I'll call you

He showed a malignant unwillingness to differentiate
frames suggesting an underlying refusal
to distinguish between performative, substantive,
substantive-performative, and perfermo-substantive
utterances.

"I thought utterances were for cows"

"You think you're big but in reality you're
very little"

"In reality" I don't exist though I will recently
have moved to Buffalo.

Elbow or buckled philodendrom

"It's just hard it's not like you're gonna get killed"

First there is the build up & then the fizz (fix).
In Utopia the story will never end.

—"Or begin"

"Yah but a softball is still hard"

Or if this followed the other, that this? This that
other, the followed this if, or.

Just don't say it like you mean it

You can't substitute *heating oil* for 'moral panic'

You get the hose, I got the biscuits

Look! Look!

I'm eternally attentive but nowhere sentient

"Just tell the snake, 'N O'!"

Fluidly floral or floridly fluid

Butcha better belch

"No they're not fighting it's real play"

She doesn't give up she doesn't even try!

Flummoxed or flunked or flushed or refrigerator

Decals make the man much the way oilcloth
makes the kitchen. "Oilcloth" being an old-
fashioned way of saying *linoleum*, "decals"
being an oblique way of suggesting *models for*.

"I'm hungry and want someone to greet"

If sand'll get you shore, sad'll get
you exactly nowhere.

"But I can't help it"

"Then I can't help you"

(As if volition were voluntary)

You have to occupy yourself sometimes, draw
on your own resources.

As if *you* had any!

My inner resources are overdrawn, in the
sense of interest due & exaggerated, which go
together like an ant and a pineapple,
a zebra and polystyrene wrap, petunia
and DOS 4.01.

DOS, DOS and not a drop to drink

DOS, DOS don't you know the road

What I've never understood about fashion is that
if you buy a new swimsuit (what we used to call
bathing suit) every summer what do you do with
the old trunks?

Ou sont les bikinis *d'antan*?

"Yeah yeah" [negative double positive]

MAKE MAYONNAISE NOT MUNITIONS

DISPOSSESS THE RICH NOT THE POOR

Save gas, stay at home.
Save electricity, sleep more.
Improve your mind, get a vasectomy.

No I'm not hostile, just unhappy.

No I'm not unhappy, just hostile.

I mean, *hospitable* . . . I mean I've been
a little grumpy the past few decades

Harder for a rich man to read a poem than
for a hippopotamus to sing bel canto.

Preposterous!

Para(pa)posterous.

Indubitably, indubitablier, emergency intubation

—But then you've probably never heard Rataxes sing!

Not only that, either—when two bits ain't
worth a dime, you might as well swap those
Swamis for some canned fish

No, I'm not sarcastic, just unsettled, like
images of the Indians trouble my sleep, like
we settled altogether too much too fast &
have to throw out our backs retracing our
steps

There is a madness to their method: Take no
prisoners, pensioners

For to dissect is to delight in the
sentient; all else is so much hocus
pocus, ring-a-leveos of repression and
triplebind, culpable blindness to what
is before our touch. Read to redress,
disguise as promise—not to submit.

Hollow words with a ring of truth,
signet of sorrow. Not to reprimand is
to be remanded to the custody of those
escaped the tide of moral pull:
accumulation beyond the wildest needs
of child or woman or man—this is
the first sin. Our jailers
are our constipating sense of self—
not that madmen claim many kin.
Rue or be ruled or take a ruler
to the wind to measure the gravity
that locates us surely as the morning
falls, whether or not we get up.

Or else—

wake me for meals

The Influence of Kinship Patterns upon Perception of an Ambiguous Stimulus

What's money worth? Not a whole lot if

You come up a few bits short & come

Away empty handed. If that was the case

What would you have to say then? At least

The motorperson knows how to blow a whistle.

At least in the winter it's not summer

(God damn mosquitoes & horseflies). What did

The Mandela say to the Mandela? BOY

HITS IGLOO. Snowed motion, i.e., frosted or

Laminated. To be such a bitter pill

& have nothing wrong. *Don't laugh*

It really hurted. If you put on

My shirt then what shirt am I

Going to wear? The kind of people

Wear plaid Bermuda shorts. The kind of

People that judge people who wear

Plaid Bermuda shorts. The kind of

Day this has been (I think I am

Falling into a tunnel of love but

Forget to get on). For a long time I'd

Say *twirl* when I meant 'spin'. Have you

Heard the one about the fly & the

Paper? The fly bottle could not found

The fly. The Mother Bear could not

Find the rest of the story. Harry has his

Troubles too but these are not interesting enough

To bear replay. "That's a very

Suspicious-looking baby." "It's hard

Not to be a baby." "But

Are there really babies or just baby-

Behavior?" —For the purpose

Of your request I'm including this

Sentence about the influence of John

Ashbery. While the packet

Boat sunk I can still imagine I am

Crawling into it; at the same time the ice

Is too thin to

Pretend to fall through.

Meanwhile, the water is wetter in the

Rich man's pond but doesn't taste

As good. —Hey wait a minute!

That's a bit *too* close, try to stay

Back *at least 10* inches. So what

If the margins don't

Turn out right? Whadda you *mean* you're

Going to the next poem? *This is the best*

Part! Oh, I'm sorry, I guess I misunderstood

You. —But nobody seems to want to hear

About the pain we men feel

Having our prerogatives questioned.

A bunch of darn-dash pragmatists

With justice on their side (for all

The good that will do them). Don't

Frame me or I'll bust you in the

Doldrums. —*Now let's*

Switch the subject & try to find

Out what's on *your* mind. Voyage of life

Getting you down? Felt better when things

Were really rocky & now there's smooth

Sailing but it's lost its meaning? I'm a

Good listener & only mildly demanding:

There's just the one-time fee (mostly

For paper & printing & distribution

Costs) & unlimited returns. I'm bubbling over

With empathy & good advice & I'm not

Afraid to tell you where I think you've

Gone wrong. Let's face it—

From the word *go* you've

Resented me—resented my being finished

In the face of your—what?—continuing

On? But I don't mean to be complete

If that makes you feel distant; still

As I say, I

Do want some distance. She was a

Sort of Betsy Ross figure but without the

Accoutrements—no washer/dryer, just the one

TV. I said to her—What can you *expect*

From a poem? —evidently a lot less than

She did. A poem bleeds

Metaphorically, just like I do. I can

No more breathe than face

The music. But if the first

Banana smells a rat look out for

Lost leader (tossed reader). —"I

don't think I'm ever

Going home." —I don't think

I've ever been home. *We are looking for*

Cheerful, enthusiastic self-starters

With solid backgrounds in detailed

Wails. The point

Not to change history but to change

Events. For instance, you

Can change in the car, change on the

Beach, or use a changing room

At the beach. Don't change me

& I won't change a hair on your

Chinny chin chin. Or let me

Put it this way: You can call

Me anything you want to but give me

The right change. That's right: I

haven't changed, you have. It's

Not the time it's the beer. I'm in

A rush, don't forget to send a

Check. Not a con

Just a dodge. Not a dodge a Lincoln-

Mercury. *Take me to your leader.* Take me

To the 5 & Dime I've got to go.

Faith under leisure: as difficult as

Keeping a hat in a hurricane

Or an appointment with an erasure.

One Mandela hit the other Mandela in the nose.

What color blood came out?

R-E-D spells *red*.

Are you people? You're about the nicest people

I know & I know some pretty unpleasant

characters.

Dark City

1 . *Apple-Picking Time*

A transom stands bound to a flagpole. Hard
by we go hardly which way is which
lingering somewhere unsettled where evidence
comes harder by sockets, stems
etched in flexed omission like osmotic
molarities flickering edge and orange at flow
rates unrepresentative of ticking or torpor
any child or person requires for, well
against, that remorse remonstration
brings. It's cold outside, maybe
but the heart sinks daily in
slump of sampled parts and *I*
feel like carelessness, disowning what's
acquired in indifferent
animation, no body swaps to—
not as if elevated or cut down
to size up, like layers of lost
boys, like aspiration in a tub
at sea, lists all the scores and
scares at measures twice the fall.
I'm parked because I have no taste
to go—penned down, no row to call

my own. *Abruptly, silently* borrowing
ignition from rumble, pouring
face into a
stir . . .
We're a great fire, pining for a
tower to burn through, yet no matter
whose ice scatters our shouts—
dive for the switches, bury the
slots.

There's an eggplant in heaven
Seen it there, know the sign
It's awaiting for me
End of time, long-lost rime

I loved my love with gold
She loved me with her smile
But I took no possession
Then / Had no taste called mine
I knew I wept alone that night
As sure as sheep in folds
The I has ways the arm betrays
For now my lance is warped

The Bitter Core o'erwhelms its fate
An abler loss casts breeze
Sobriety's a fool's way out
I'll take the sea in me, in me
Nor swap the waves for thee.

Floorlength gowns of commodious indelicacy
suffusing articles on plums
in monk's applause, equipped with attenuated
slips, adjunctive rumination, felt
bellows. Before I, in the interests of
but not to further ascribe, at which
mechanism, slate, pediment, protrusion

abutment, laceration, absinthe-oriented
divestment gaged to occur or unveil
its numinous ectoplasmic Jill or gel or
JELLO AGAIN THIS IS JACK BENNY FOR
JELLO PUDDING AND PIE FILLING.
Overboard or just over-by-a-long
shot. Grateful to even imagine
shore.

> As a matter of fact
> I'm as good as packed.
> I slept longer than you
> Now isn't that true?

A poem should not mean but impale
not be but bemoan,
                    boomerang
buck(le)
        bubble. Malted meadows & hazelnut
innuendos: I'll bet the soda water
gets the shakes sooner than
Dan gets to Tampa. "Don't Tampa
with me or I'll lacerate that
evisceration off your face so fast
you'll think my caddle prod was a
lollipop." "Stay out my face or I'll
deploy my assets against whatever
collateral you've got left after I
target your abstemious alarm." He
was the kind of guy who pushed
my buttons but couldn't carry a
tune from Kuala Lampur to
Guadalajuara, like those zebras
with cross hatchings, or the trapeze
family with Venusian ventilators. I
mean I felt good at first
but then it dawned on me, what

if it was really a mistake, maybe
I shouldn't have said what I
said, did what I
done. Mildred paced around the museum
for another few hours before she spotted
him, but it was much too crowded to
finish the job right there. "They were
my favorite boots," she cried. "They are
your only boots," I replied.

2. *Early Frost*

I think it's time we let the cat out
its bag, swung the dog over the
shoulder, so to say, let the hens
say "hey" to the woodpeckers, doled
out some omniaversions to the
too-tapped-upon, the tethers without
toggles, the field-happy expeditioneers
on the march to Tuscaloosa, Beloit,
Manual Falls, Florid Oasis.
"Damn but you're a beautiful
cow / of a / bell! Haven't
I seen you on the radio?"
Where are those fades (arcades, shades)
when you need them? Who
was that text I saw you with
last night? Is there life after
grammar (glamour)? The Czech
is in the jail (the wreck is
in the wail, the deck is in the
sail, the Burma shave's shining over the
starry blue skies, Waukeegan, New Jersey,
1941). *He that cannot pay: let him pay!*
She that peeps through a hole will kiss
the wave that troubled her. No larder

but has its puddle, no rose without
overthrows. Ask no questions and at last
you shall be blind! A stumble may
prevent a fall but a fall guy's
my kind of man. Every poem
has its price, every anxiety its reward—
but no person ever tripped in the same
place more than *I* choose to
recall. There are spots even on the
sofa (meddle not with another person's
meddling, i.e., the rock that falls
from the sky breaks your toes).
For the footprint makes the joint a
well-appointed appurtenance aside the
jesting hooligan, shenanigan, or
general call to bedlam, or did
she say, *be calm*? Clammy hands
hurt the advancement of the waiter
but I never heard no tell of no
gust or gallon of time worth the
curing in weight alone. Boxers
can't live by punching alone, but
stay clear of such as possible—a
Divine Swerve will still land you
in Hell's cauldron. *Thus*
make your peace with yourself at
your own risk for peace with the Devil
costs everybody more than you could
hope to destroy. *Holy is as holy does.*
Essence precludes existence.

3. *Endless Destination*

If I should die
cut out my throat
and burn it on the pyre
of their indifference.
It means no more to me
than that, to take
your hand in my
hand and turn our backs
from the wreck
not of our lives
but where we have been given
to live them. I would not
walk alone here, where the
dark surrounds, where your face
radiates beyond my swollen
misgivings and clarifies the mist
of my belonging. Stay near
that I may hold you lightly
else the fear inside tear
away what measures I have
held against the night.

Love's no more than that
a straw against the wind
that blows us to the ground
without submission. Come
love, come, take this
shadow I call me: cast
it against stone, lest the gloom
become us. Come cast me
down 'gainst shore, where
sand enfolds us.

Love is like love, a baby
like a baby, meaning like
memory, light like light.
A journey's a detour
and a pocket a charm
in which deceits are borne.
A cloud is a cloud and
a story like a story,
song is a song, fury
like fury.

4. *In the Pink*

Now let's turn to some advise for expectant
fathers. Never wear a hat to a
hanging or carry a feather pillow to
cello practice. Suffer not the
professor of culture nor the minister
of taste, but assail all who
complacent sit in the place of those
deserve it. Take the cracks on
the wall as your credo or call—
obscurity's in the eye of
ones will not behold—
what they can understand
isn't worth the price of
a used tin can. I may be loco
but at least I listen: What
you've tuned out would make a Paradise
of Plies.

This is the difference between truth
and reality: the one advertises itself
in the court of brute circumstance
the other is framed by its own
insistences. Truth's religious, reality

cultural, or rather
truth is the ground of reality's
appearance but reality intervenes
against all odds.

5. *The Plight of the Bumblebee*

She was a rudder
without anchor
in a chaos
of expectation,
a comb
without teeth, a
brush without
bristles.

6. [untitled]

"The words
come out of
her heart
& into the
language"
& the language
is in the heart
of that girl
who is in the heart
of you.

Charles Bernstein was born in 1950 in New York City. He attended the Bronx High School of Science and Harvard College. He lives in Buffalo, and in Manhattan, with painter Susan Bee and their children Emma and Felix.

Bernstein's first book, *Parsing,* was published by his own Asylum's Press in 1976. In 1978 he began editing, with Bruce Andrews, the influential critical journal, *L=A=N=G=U=A=G=E.* The same year, Sun & Moon Press published *Shade,* in its first book publication. *Controlling Interests* (1980) and *Islets/Irritations* (1983) further established the characteristic range of Bernstein's stylistic and philosophic preoccupations. *The Sophist,* published in 1987, made apparent that comedy was a fundamental element of his work.

Like *The Sophist, Rough Trades,* published in 1981, received international critical attention. Writing in *American Book Review* Pierre Joris declared: "*Rough Trades*—and starting with the title's witty punning on atmospheric conditions, sexuality, labor relations—does not only give pleasure through its intelligence and wit. It is also a book that demands the reader's constant rethinking of her own 'ground' and poetic presuppositions.... This is exhilarating and liberating work."

Bernstein has published two substantial, and widely reviewed, collections of essays—*Content's Dream* (1986) and *A Poetics* (1992). In 1990, he edited *The Politics of Poetic Form: Poetry and Public Policy* as well as *Patterns / Contexts / Time,* with Phillip Foss. He has also edited collections of poetry for *The Paris Review* and *boundary 2.*

In collaboration with Susan Bee, Bernstein has produced several books that explore visual settings of text. Bernstein is also active in musical theater; he has written three librettos with composer Ben Yarmolinsky.

From the early '70s to the late '80s, Bernstein worked as a writer/editor on healthcare and medical topics, with a break to serve as Associate Director of the CETA Artists Project (the largest postwar American public employment program for artists).

In 1990, Bernstein was appointed David Gray Professor of Poetry and Letters at the State University of New York, Buffalo, where he is a founding member of the Poetics Program in the Department of English.

SUN & MOON CLASSICS

The Sun & Moon Classics is a publicly supported, nonprofit program to publish new editions, translations, or republications of outstanding world literature of the late nineteenth and twentieth centuries. Through its publication of living authors as well as great masters of the century, the series attempts to redefine what usually is meant by the idea of a "classic" by dehistoricizing the concept and embracing a new, ever changing literary canon.

Organized by the Contemporary Arts Educational Project, Inc., a nonprofit corporation, and published by its program Sun & Moon Press, the series is made possible, in part, by grants and individual contributions.

This book was made possible, in part, through matching grants from the National Endowment for the Arts and from the California Arts Council, through an organizational grant from the Andrew W. Mellon Foundation, through a grant for advertising and promotion from the Lila Wallace/Reader's Digest Fund, and through contributions from the following individuals:

Charles Altieri (Seattle, Washington)
John Arden (Galway, Ireland)
Jesse Huntley Ausubel (New York, New York)
Dennis Barone (West Hartford, Connecticut)
Jonathan Baumbach (Brooklyn, New York)
Guy Bennett (Los Angeles, California)
Bill Berkson (Bolinas, California)
Steve Benson (Berkeley, California)
Charles Bernstein and Susan Bee (New York, New York)
Sherry Bernstein (New York, New York)
Dorothy Bilik (Silver Spring, Maryland)
Bill Corbett (Boston, Massachusetts)
Fielding Dawson (New York, New York)
Robert Crosson (Los Angeles, California)
Tina Darragh and P. Inman (Greenbelt, Maryland)
David Detrich (Los Angeles, California)
Christopher Dewdney (Toronto, Canada)
Philip Dunne (Malibu, California)
George Economou (Norman, Oklahoma)
Elaine Equi and Jerome Sala (New York, New York)
Lawrence Ferlinghetti (San Francisco, California)
Richard Foreman (New York, New York)
Howard N. Fox (Los Angeles, California)
Jerry Fox (Aventura, Florida)

In Memoriam: Rose Fox
Melvyn Freilicher (San Diego, California)
Miro Gavran (Zagreb, Croatia)
Peter Glassgold (Brooklyn, New York)
Barbara Guest (New York, New York)
Perla and Amiram V. Karney (Bel Air, California)
Fred Haines (Los Angeles, California)
Fanny Howe (La Jolla, California)
Harold Jaffe (San Diego, California)
Ira S. Jaffe (Albuquerque, New Mexico)
Alex Katz (New York, New York)
Tom LaFarge (New York, New York)
Mary Jane Lafferty (Los Angeles, California)
Michael Lally (Santa Monica, California)
Norman Lavers (Jonesboro, Arkansas)
Jerome Lawrence (Malibu, California)
Stacey Levine (Seattle, Washington)
Herbert Lust (Greenwich, Connecticut)
Norman MacAffee (New York, New York)
Rosemary Macchiavelli (Washington, DC)
Beatrice Manley (Los Angeles, California)
Martin Nakell (Los Angeles, California)
Toby Olson (Philadelphia, Pennsylvania)
Maggie O'Sullivan (Hebden Bridge, England)
Rochelle Owens (Norman, Oklahoma)
Marjorie and Joseph Perloff (Pacific Palisades, California)
Dennis Phillips (Los Angeles, California)
David Reed (New York, New York)
Ishmael Reed (Oakland, California)
Janet Rodney (Santa Fe, New Mexico)
Joe Ross (Washington, DC)
Dr. Marvin and Ruth Sackner (Miami Beach, Florida)
Floyd Salas (Berkeley, California)
Tom Savage (New York, New York)
Leslie Scalapino (Oakland, California)
James Sherry (New York, New York)
Aaron Shurin (San Francisco, California)
Charles Simic (Strafford, New Hampshire)
Gilbert Sorrentino (Stanford, California)
Catharine R. Stimpson (Staten Island, New York)
John Taggart (Newburg, Pennsylvania)
Nathaniel Tarn (Tesuque, New Mexico)

Fiona Templeton (New York, New York)
Mitch Tuchman (Los Angeles, California)
Wendy Walker (New York, New York)
Anne Walter (Carnac, France)
Arnold Wesker (Hay on Wye, England)

If you would like to be a contributor to this series, please send your tax-deductible contribution to The Contemporary Arts Educational Project, Inc., a non-profit corporation, 6026 Wilshire Boulevard, Los Angeles, California 90036.

BOOKS IN THE SUN & MOON CLASSICS

*First American publication
**Revised edition